KV-000-469

LISTENING
TO
DIFFERENT
DRUMMERS

BIRMINGHAM LIBRARY SERVICES
DISCARD

by

CIARAN O'DRISCOLL

DEDALUS

The Dedalus Press
24 The Heath,
Cypress Downs,
Dublin 6W
Ireland

© 1993 Ciaran O'Driscoll

ERDINGTON LIBRARY
BIRMIN   M B24 9HP

ISBN 1873790376   er)
ISBN   nd)

Cover design by David Hanamy

Dedalus Press Books are represented and distributed
abroad by Password, 23 New Mount St.,
Manchester M4 4DE.

The Dedalus Press receives financial assistance from An
Chomhairle Ealaíon, The Arts Council, Ireland.

Printed in Ireland by Colour Books Ltd.

For my Parents

ACKNOWLEDGEMENTS

Some of these poems appeared originally in the following publications: *Cyphers, Dedalus Editions 4, Dedalus Irish Poets, Fortnight, The Irish Times, The Kilkenny Anthology, On the Counterscarp: Limerick Writing 1961-1991, The Poetry Ireland Review, Thistledown: Poems for UNICEF*.

I am grateful to the Netherlands Embassy and the Netherlands Business Association for the James Joyce Prize which enabled me to visit the Netherlands in 1989; to Aer Lingus and An Chomhairle Ealaíon for facilitating a visit to the United States in 1991; and to the Heinrich Böll Foundation for a residency in the Heinrich Böll Cottage, Achill, February 1993.

"Voices of South Africa" was originally part of "Voices and Light", a performance by the Fourfront Poets in the Belltable, Limerick, in December 1989. There are a number of allusions in the poem to material found in Chapters III and IV of *South Africa An Historical Introduction* by Freda Troup (London, 1972).

"A Moment Under Siege" was written for Daghdha Dance Company on the occasion of Limerick's Treaty 300 celebrations, 1991. It was performed in the context of Daghdha's dance-drama "Through an Eye of Stone" at the Dublin Theatre Festival, 1991, and elsewhere.

The District Nurse (Part 1 of "Astronomy Lessons") was prompted by a report on Cambodia by Justin O'Brien in *The Irish Times* of 12 February 1992.

"Line's Odyssey" was written for the catalogue of David Lilburn's exhibition of monoprints "Home Ground", 1991.

In "To an Empty Coke Can", *ourodoxeio* is the Greek for a chamber pot; in "Friesland Sequence", *moeilijk* is the Dutch for "difficult", "hard", and Davies is a character from Erskine Childers' *The Riddle of the Sands*; in "Getting Away", the "falling rocks" are not rocks which fall, but rocks from which Druids are supposed to have jumped to their deaths, to rejoin the cycle of reincarnation (cf. *Jamaica Inn* by Daphne du Maurier).

CONTENTS

5. TOWARDS THE END AND THE BEGINNING

6. BACK HOME

1. AT HOME ....

CHAMPAGNE IN THE AFTERNOON

(for Conor, born 17 April 1989)

Champagne in the afternoon and ploughed fields:
a baby holding wisdom in his fist
has come to sit in our assembly,
an elder statesman wise as a crow's nest.

Champagne in the afternoon and ploughed fields;
and in trees that have yet to spring a leaf,
a staggered procession of crows' nests
erected without planning permission
overnight, as if for once
some truly positive disaster, sheep
beneath them with their gifts of lambs.

Champagne in the afternoon and ploughed fields
as through the thrown-down land a train
ploughs me towards welcoming a statesman child
who sits in love's assembly
and has so much to learn, he must
be gift-bearer supreme, ambassador
of life's fulness: so with impunity,
once in a lifetime, among lambs and nests,
I'm drinking champagne in the afternoon.

Such a perennial cliché, the once
in a lifetime experience
of being a father for the first time!
The ironic anaesthetist
told Margaret she'd feel no pain,
only a feeling of fulness: what fulness
do I experience in this express
that ploughs me through the midlands home,
induced by more, much more than this champagne,
this afternoon of ploughed fields and crows' nests!

Crows' nests in the intricacies of branches
precise as a japanese print,
and a train that ploughs me through the midlands earth
to a child with everything to learn
who already looks so wise.
Like the contractions of childbirth
these verses seem to have no end,
but finally there's an announcement:
life, having been tried to the utmost,
is determined to continue; I've read
it in my child ambassador's
caput of black hair, his dented head;
and in his tiny fist, which is the fist
of afternoon champagne, ploughed fields, crows' nests.

ENVOY

In the person of this diminutive
envoy, God has installed himself in state
under the canopy of a carry-cot
in the spare room. Each morning now I rise
and stagger out of bed with a dry cough
after a sleep of three or four hours:
you could say I have developed an ear
for the opaque and deafening pronouncements
of an incontinent ambassador
who needs new underclothes before breakfast.
Having pissed on yesterday's yellow suit,
he'll issue today's ultimata in green,
his throat the duct through which God's word is passed
to us, and we pour propitiation.

POEM FOR A "MIDNIGHT MUSE" READING

(at the Belltable, Limerick)

All of us here tonight including
the man standing on the stairs
unsure if he's in the right place,
keeping an option on freedom open;

all of us here including those
with an ear for the sound of drink
who came because time had been called;

those who came to see and be seen
and those who support the arts;
insomniacs; lovers of poetry
who live forever in hope;

those who got in without paying
and those who, with or without
the required status, paid the reduced price;
those who have fallen out
with lovers, avoiding empty beds;
those who brought lovers along
for an aesthetic experience
and a few pricey glasses of wine;

those who glow in the warmth of conversation
between the acts; those whom the music makes
garrulous; those who pull bored faces
and sigh with impatience when poets read;
those who think a child of five
could write better poetry than this;

all of us here tonight including those
who intended to come but were waylaid;
those who are wisely asleep
in hope of the proverb's promised health and wealth;
nightwalkers watched from a car
with a blue light revolving on its roof;
guardians of order; guardians of chaos;

all of us here including
the poet who wants a word in your ear
have so much in common when the chips are down,

when with the press of a button
darkness gulps down the picture on the screen
or the night's last mouthful is gulped down
and the barman had taken to beating
the floor with the handletop of his broom
and we're pitched out under the open sky
once more, incoherent under the crescent moon,
and with no desire to go home;

so much in common that secretly
the butcher wishes his days
not to end before he writes
his poetry of carcasses,
the red varieties of meats
lined on hooks in his freezers,
and the bus conductor a poem
about the varieties of faces;

and at the innermost calling of time
there's a poem like a crescent moon,
a child, on everyone's shoulder,
a poem that cannot sleep,
a poem that cries in a basket
abandoned on a railway station bench.

FOREST

When, as I often do, I think of those
primal perceptions lost to sight
now in the mazes of artifice –
unprocessable, nameless things that cannot
be freeze-dried or committed to a page,
provoking memories, aftermaths
of pure experience – I image
a forest standing forever aloof
from a riot of chainsaws that feeds
an endless printout of verbiage
or coffee not tasting on a dull
morning like a mush of cereals,
the fresh-ground mountain beans of life
instead of its desiccated granules.

THIS SILENCE

All afternoon there hasn't been a sound
that's capable of breaking this silence,
no loophole in it that permits enquiry.

– The sounds on the periphery don't count:
the whoosh of warm air from the heater,
deceleration and acceleration
of traffic at the nearby roundabout.

Consider the pulverising power of this
silence, its steamroller of absent sounds:
redundant phone and letter box, doorbell
that doesn't know the sound of its own ringing.
– The coalman doesn't count, as neither do
countless collectors for charities,
nor begging and blessing traveller women:
heater, cars, coalman, beggars count as silence.

I wonder will there ever be a match
for this silence, a sound important enough
to break it. Hours later I'm still wondering,
filling pages with words besteeped in silence.

– Meanwhile the traveller women beg and bless me
and the coalman passes the time of day
and money changes hands in the doorway
and the redundant doorbell rings its silence
and cars negotiate the roundabout
and warm air is blown from the heater
and time is permeated and engulfed.

This silence is a rusted scaffold left
to stand after the building of communion
had been abandoned, or a skeleton
sitting on the floor of an empty room
waiting in cobwebs for the postman
to deliver his consignment of flesh
which has been seized by customs, or someone
prepared to wait forever for something
that's so important nothing else could count.

(To what depths of disgruntlement we may
descend has yet to be determined:
this is a coalface where
no hooter blows after the longest shift.)

2. ... IN THE LAND OF INERTIA

SUPERMARKET

They've blood-let Mozart in the Meat Department
to make black pudding: hence the anemia
of *nacht-musak* that fills the air
and the floating sensation in my head.

Eternities of self-replacing goods,
forever sold, forever on display,
confront me as I hover dreamily
on winged ankles an inch above the floor.

Only the creaking of a trolley's rollers
returns me to reality:
the soft footpad of the shopping beast
stalking his chicken pieces, beans and bread.

TIME AND THE CHEESE-CUTTER

The cheese-cutter is old and growing older
every minute: she grits her teeth
and tugs until I'm afraid
the wire will slice into her skinny hand.
But she'll die or pierce the rind
of this round farmhouse cheese.

To think I could have asked for any other –
Double Gloucester with chives, or Cheddar,
Wensleydale, Gouda or Gruyere,
Brie or Red Leicester – they're all here
in neatly-wrapped accessible portions ...

and now the cheese-cutter's refused
the help of her white-coated assistant,
a fat man with florid features
who hovers, limp with embarrassment,

as this drama gathers an audience
from the bread department and the meat;
this contest between an ageing woman
and the tough rind of a farmhouse cheese,

this time-consuming tragi-comedy
that has buried my head in the crook of my arm
on the glass top of the cooler,
recalling all the afternoons I've lost
since my piercing of the natal round,
is even attracting window-gazers.

But the old woman growing older
with every second reassures me:
"As soon as I get through the rind,"
she says, "the rest will be plain sailing";
and once more lifts a knife to cut
a deeper groove for the slipping wire.

"It's lucky you're not in a hurry," she says
through gritted teeth as she tugs, and the girl
at the bread counter stifles a titter.
I lean my head on the glass of the cooler,
watching mould grow on Cambazola.

INSANITY VIEW

I live at No 1 Insanity View,
and Freddie Bottomly's next door to me
at No 3.
He has a goatee beard and recently
he bought a wheelbarrow.
"Nice wheelbarrow," I say,
and he grins with childish delight.
I'll murder him some night.

And I'll kill and eat old Mrs Fox
who lives across the road at No 2
and thought of nothing, towards the end of the war,
only the V - 2
and whether it would blast her window box
of petunias and primulas
into eternity. And of course
there's Mr and Mrs Wilberforce

living at No 4
with their three nasty children
who knock at my front door
and run: I fancy they're tougher to chew
than Mr Bottomly's wheelbarrow,
but I'll kill and eat them too.
Aye, and everybody else
who lives on Insanity View.

TO AN EMPTY COKE CAN

Thou long-ravished cohabitee
of tawdriness; thou foster-child
of laziness and the lack of any bin
in close proximity to this toilet!
Empty coke can that canst thus remain
undisturbèd on the ledge above the door
leading to the skylighted inner sanctum
of the plastic-seated *ourodoxeio*
whereon I oft would surreptitiously
smoke-puffing sit in periods before
reluctant lectures in Sociology
to even more reluctant art students,
hiding away from them a while, debating
whether to feign sickness and escape
or stand my ground in the forlorn hope
some ray out of my dimness might pen'trate
a skull of less than general density!
Here did I leave thee then, some years ago,
after a lecture during which thou wert
both slaker of my dry discursive thirst,
and mine instant symbol of mass culture –
thou, drunken from by everyone from bums
in railway station doors to presidents,
now empty, gath'ring dust unvisited
by any but whose eyes don't stray above
the middle line of vision, or if they do,
see thee but heed thee not! And yet thou standst
somehow a potent symbol of th'inertia
of lecturers, jakes-cleaners, caretakers
in th'idle fantasies of their self-absorbed
generations, who have not taken thee
from thine exalted perch of mockery
and crumpled thee for daring to reproach

their sad insuperable listlessness,
nor, finding a far bin to throw thee in,
have said, "Thus perish as thy throwaway
nature dictates, insolent deviant
seeking this niche of immortality
from whence t'expose the contradiction of
our indisposable disposables;
flaunting, to haunt our guilty lassitude,
the unbiodegradability
by which thou cloggest streams, defacest beaches
and litterest the planet everywhere."

MANGOES

Something about them goes against the grain
of our sodden, sainted land:
as if our farmers were ever in need
of anything but rain,
or our priests wore golden robes and prayed
for sunshine – and were heard.

Their very presence on fruitstalls is
an occasion of sin:
think of the succulent yellow mess
inside a mango's skin
inviting us to sell our birthright
of guilt and deprivation for a fruit.

Or imagine the mouth of misery
dripping a yellow-gold reminder
of generous climates, cloudless skies,
the heresy of an earthly paradise!
(We're lucky the price of them rules out
the theory that they're a communist plot.)

CONCERNING LATCHICOES

Some say the word is from
the Irish, but I like to think it came
from *latch*, to *latch on* to someone:
a big bollux with an inane grin
in a pub, who before you know
is telling you his life story. Someone
who latches on to you and won't let go
is what *I* understand by *latchico*,
and I have forgotten its Irish root
as often as it has been explained to me.
In this respect my idea of what
a latchico is is itself a latchico.
Another latchico of an idea
of mine is that there's always one,
and always only one, in any given
pub. Latchico-resources
are the only resources in the country
that are evenly distributed. Besides
being difficult if not impossible
to shake off, another enduring trait
of latchicoes is their propensity
to repetition: punch lines of bad jokes,
explanations of bad jokes ("D'ya get it? Hah?"),
portentously misquoted lines of verse,
What the Taoiseach said to me the day I had
a few pints with him in the Shelbourne Bar,
What "Sam" or "Paddy" told me on his death-bed,
the three degrees of female circumcision
in graphic detail, all of these and more
are flogged to their reiterated deaths
in the eardrums of random victims by
the nation's task-force of latchicoes.
I used to make a distinction between
the *Latchico Vulgaris* and the more
refined breed that stops short of smutty jokes,

bad language, shouting and ultimate insult,
but this quibble is dangerous in practice:
the *Latchico Rarus* is hard to detect
in the first stages of conversation,
and may have administered a lethal dose
of boredom before the victim even suspects.
My research on how to recognize latchicoes
is not far advanced because in common with
a lot of other noxious forms of life
they have the capacity to take on
the colours of their habitat, and change
with fashion and the seasons. However,
a few pointers are worth noting: beware
the seemingly self-contained hulk on the barstool
beside you who suddenly turns and says
Excuse me. Haven't I met you somewhere before?
Or, more subtly, the gentle but firm hand
on the shoulder, the ingratiating voice
that croons *Excuse me, Sir, but you look like
an educated man ...* Your response to such
openings should be a sudden clutching of your crotch
and a beeline for the jakes, or the sighting
of a long lost relative in the furthest reaches
of the bar. Finally, a latchico
never thinks he is himself a latchico,
so when you've managed, after great effort,
to shake off one, don't be fooled by the next
(there's always a few floating, on holiday),
who comes to pat you on the back, and say
*By God, but some people can't leave a man
alone, can they now? They have no regard
for your need of a bit of privacy.
Isn't that a fact? Isn't it true for me?*

Hah?

LAST KNOWN SIGHTING OF HOMO SAPIENS: ACHILL ISLAND, 24 FEBRUARY 1993

Hijacked by teenage guerrillas escaped from school –
the prettiest one up front, on the ledge of the windscreen,
conveying the orders of High Command to the driver –
suddenly, megaphonically, the bus began to blare
the music of the Daily Late Afternoon Revolution,

and shards of mystic landscape fell around in my head,
crevasses opened in ribbed bracken hillsides
swallowing sheep and cows, the solemn cloud-puncturing peaks
of mountains began to sweat blood and spew guts:
in a split second all was dementia,
and all that wasn't dementia was claustrophobia.

What's the matter with the Youth of Today? I asked myself
while the Youth of Today sat unabashed on one another's knees
as if sexual candour had only just been invented,
and compared notes on the latest release
by Hydraulic Drills or Black-and-Decker Convention;
You're getting to be a bit of an old fogey, I said to myself
*It has crept up on you unbeknownst, this
eminently pensionable desire for beauty and peace,
for the sublime in nature and old-fashioned solitude.*

But to tell the truth, for the previous hour or more,
my enjoyment of the landscape had been marred
by an increasingly urgent desire to micturate
and that was how I came to be so privileged,
to be the one who sighted once again,
after so many years, a specimen
of *homo sapiens*; because
when next the bus pulled in to drop
newspapers outside a shop,
I got out of my seat and elbowed my way
through a thicket of adolescent foreplay
to ask the driver *An bhfuil cead agam dul amach?*
and sprinted down the footpath to a pub,

and there he was!
I caught my first glimpse of him as I opened the door,
an old creature with a hooked nose, who was seated
not in front of, but *under* the television,
and facing out towards an ambivalent audience.
He was talking loudly and gesticulating about God knows what
in competition with the Minister for Finance
who was lacing the thin gruel of budgetary rectitude,
no doubt, with a potent narcotic of buzz-phrases,
Kick-starting the Economy and Putting Structures
in Place for Better Things in the Pipeline
which are not, however, Feasible at This Point in Time.

I was in too much of a hurry to listen
to the old creature, but on my way back out
I confirmed the primal fact that he was not only *not*
watching television, but *competing* with it,

and while there are many species that don't watch television
such as seagulls, penguins, polar bears and tigers,
there is only one species on this earth that has been known
to be capable of actively competing with it, namely
the story-telling conversation-making species of *homo sapiens*
believed by many to be long extinct; but I can now aver
it still survives in at least one particular instance,
this king Canute trying to roll back the amnesiac waves
that lap the shores of our quotidian consciousness,
this Sisyphus forever pushing the boulder of truth
up the implacable slopes of Whizz-Kid Hill.

For the truth is that our whole mutated race
could be born again as human beings if only we tried
talking to one another, entertaining one another
in the places where we live; that culture, knowledge and ideas
are not things that can be pre-packaged and distributed
to the masses by patronizing central agencies;

and that television itself can and should be used to encourage
our participatory natures and not to lull and deaden us.

So there it is, the last known sighting of *homo sapiens*
on Achill Island, 24 February 1993,
Ash Wednesday and Budget Day, point of coincidence
between ecclesiastical and political calendars,
a day of belt-tightening in both secular and spiritual
realms – and I was back in the bus, a bearded neanderthal,
impotent savant among the flower of hip *jeunesse*
qui pourraient mais hélas! ne savent pas, the door
of my privacy assailed once more
by a battering-ram of rock music
on the majestic fringes of the Atlantic,

heading to Heinrich Böll Cottage, Dugort, where now I am
writing it all down under a ghost's inspiration
for the lost honour of Katharina Blum.

OPEN LETTER

Dear Salman,
You probably don't know who we are –
at least you didn't know before
we took the opportunism to write
this open letter in the *Irish Aeons*
to you, about your plight.
We hope one of the few
apprised of your latest hiding place
will show it to you.
But whether *you* read it or not
this letter will further the cause
of reminding *others* who *we* are.
People are so forgetful! We must
jump at anything that will keep
our names in the limelight.
Forgive us, but it's just
the time of year when you can do
your lessers a favour or two
by sticking to your guns
in the face of a death sentence
(if you'll forgive the inept metaphor).
In exchange for recalling attention
to your persecution,
you'll give us free publicity.
All this talk about blasphemy!
Surely the worst sin among us hacks
is failing to scratch one another's backs.
And we could tell you a thing or two
about back-scratching's infinite regress:
the thing is never to draw the line.
A pity you didn't know in time
that those who wield power love to join
with writers in the endless game,
and that the least you can do,
if you don't want to scratch, is not to tear:

31

remain innocuous, or be obscure;
don't spell the fucking thing out
or we'll all be in the shit!
Who wants to be famous and manhunted,
lionized and dead?
Therefore I'm sure you'll understand
that when we, the Writers of Ireland
Muted by Political Savagery –
WIMPS for short – organize a reading
in your honour, we intend
to read *our own* works, not *yours*.
You never know what fanatic glowers,
gun hidden, from the back of an audience
that seems to be uniformly polite
and fearful we're going to drone on past midnight.

THE SNAILS

The snails, essentially aliens, having
established themselves in the lax period
of the interregnum (when nobody shat
on the throne), enjoyed such privileges as were
commensurate with and indeed beyond
citizenship (even to the extent
of devouring true citizens), and continued
to increase in insolence until at last
these bandits lay in wait on every tree
in the kingdom. In the inner councils
of the new regime, for several months,
various personal troubles had absorbed
whatever beleaguered energy remained
between one sleep and another after
much wrangling over decisions which succeeded
in postponing for twenty-four hours more
the perpetually imminent collapse
of the entire economic unit.
And during all this time the snails
consolidated their illegitimate claims
on everything outside the palace doors,
and posted sentries in the nooks of walls
that bordered the kingdom. Then came the rains,
and the snails multiplied, and intrepid knights
who had formerly ventured into the open
and even dared to cut an odd snail down
from the perch of its bloated *hubris,* and smash
it underfoot, no longer went outside,
and all within grew tired of listening
to the sound of their own pompous voices
reiterating jaded remedies
for the world's ills, while the world itself
became increasingly a world of snails:

citizens would wake to find a left arm
or right leg gone, eaten away, and a trail
of silver on their beds, slimy snail-issue
shared the children's beds, giving them the kiss
of death, and disgustingly swollen slugs
were rumoured to be hiding within the palace
itself, to have penetrated as far
as the king's chamber, where he sat on his throne.
Finally the chancellor of the exchequer,
who had taken to drink during the crisis,
was ignominiously dismissed for using
the palace funds to finance his habit,
and a more abstemious successor managed
over a period of several weeks
to save three pounds and eighty-eight pennies,
enough to engage the services of
a mountebank with magic remedies
reputed to be quelling like scourges
in neighbouring realms. Sitting on his throne,
the king has spoken: "Desperate diseases",
he says, "have need of desperate remedies."
The chancellor of the exchequer holds
her breath, as does the whole privy council:
under the cover of fall of evening,
at the very hour when crawling plunderers
will gird themselves the most to crawl and plunder,
a few worthies, chosen for ruthlessness,
run to and fro, describing magic circles
in pure white powder round the citizens' homes.

3. THE MYTH OF THE SOUTH

THE MYTH OF THE SOUTH

1. The Myth Of The South

It is true that in the South there is, in general,
an absence of agency – I mean of the efficient sort.
Things somehow *get* done, if you know what I mean.
But things could just as easily *not* get done.
Things happen according to the seasons,
and even then they depend on mood, which depends
in turn on the weather. The people of the South –
even in bigger towns, such as Li-Chung and Li-Cho –
lack any sense of urgency, they haven't yet
pulled themselves out of the benignly lazy state
that natural cycles warrant in a generous climate.
(Apples taste sweeter in the orchards round Li-Cho
than anywhere on earth. The children's cheeks
are as rosy as the cheeks of the apples.)
When the Emperor comes on his five-yearly visit
there's something of a flurry, but it would look
to Northerners like a Day of Rest: people can be seen
out painting their houses or fixing wagon wheels;
again, of course, depending on the weather.
The women are more beautiful in the South;
sensuous, fun-loving, they make bad secretaries;
not that there's much need of secretaries
in Li-Chung or Li-Cho. It's said the healthy lustre
of Southern people's skin comes from bathing under
the many waterfalls, which they do all day in good weather.
Very few people here except state functionaries –
usually recruited from the North – are able to write:
poetry is indistinguishable from song, although
the songs have the epic quality of being endless,
which suits the temperament and is indifferent
to the weather: when they can't sing out of doors,
in their traditional wine-gardens, they sing indoors,
in their traditional wine-taverns. The one thing
they do with great gusto is to sing.

37

Singing has no social function of the kind
the Emperor's anthropologists seem to think
must be latent under any manifest activity;
there's no *hiatus* between life and singing,
but that is not to say, as might be said
by one of our pretentious litterateurs,
hell-bent on poetry as celebration,
that singing is life for them, as life is singing.
Between songs, there's always a period
for conversation, or in the case of wakes,
for silence. New songs are composed
almost every day, and either enter the repertoire
or don't: the only critics are the singers,
which means the people, whose final verdict
is to sing or not to sing. This may all strike you
as being egregiously mindless, as it did me at first,
but I found out that they discuss their songs
with one another in the throes of composition
rather than *post factum*, and they say,
Better to make sure the wine is good
than to drink it and make a bitter face.
In this way, they ensure that very few
of the songs composed are dropped as unsingable,
and it means that their repertoire is infinite
and that everything that happens is sung about,
as well as the possible and the fantastic;
their political debates, even, occur
as an exchange of songs. Apart from that,
and the apples, the naked bodies under waterfalls,
the apple-cheeked children, the births, the funerals,
the slow creaking of cartwheels towards the huge
granaries of Li-Chung and Li-Cho; as I said,
apart from beauty and ease, love, death, and apple-wine,
nobody *does* anything here in the South;
things somehow *get* done, if you know what I mean.

2. The Myth Of The Capital

At this stage, as we take the air nightly
along the battlements of the Plague Wall, we hear
persistent rumours that the country is well again;
or at least its greater part; these rumours come
from the alcoholic wretches who are denied entry,
shouting from the bottom of the granite face
out of the rags and tatters of hearsay,
speaking of the second city and even the third,
where they say builders are busy and trade and commerce
thriving: they have heard new songs, they say,
and their feeble renditions float up to us
full of *hopes* and *loves* and *prides*; many of them
appear to be songs of building, and sound almost –
well – accomplished; a source of much amusement
as we take the air on the ramparts of the Plague
after dinner, before theatre or recital.
There is *so much* happening in the capital
these days, especially with the strolling players
and troubadours confined within the walls,
it is scarcely possible to chronicle all
that happens in one night, let alone a year.
With each new songster on the street, each new jester
or troup of wits appearing in the halls,
the importance of living in this place and time
becomes more evident. Surrounded by such ramparts,
the capital has defined itself against the country
which, ravaged by plague, may send its deceitful
emissaries no further than the butt
of this granite face on whose flat forehead we walk,
the post-prandial arbiters of taste, with our high task
of myth-making and exclusion, discrimination.
Rumours persist, as rumours will, of well-being
no further from us than a bumsore day's journey,

but by remaining wisely within these walls,
we not only protect ourselves from contamination –
which were surely a selfish thing, could it be shown
with any certainty that these fables,
concocted by desperate adventurers, had some substance –
but rather we protect our high office, which is,
as I said, taste and discrimination,
and the embattled ascendancy of the capital.

3. *Fragment Of An Account Of The North*

                            ... a brief blaze of corn
in the middle of the year, like nothing else.
A sudden busyness of people harvesting,
when all the feuding is forgotten
under the Sign of the Melting Glacier. In spring
the lost possessions tumble out of melting ice;
inventories are made at that time of the year;
the next of kin of swallowed, regurgitated houses
are informed and travel through sudden valleys
to claim their own: the neatly-tagged, preserved bodies
are quickly buried, and the mourners make the Sign
of the Melting Glacier on their foreheads, and then
get down to the serious business of haggling
about who owns what; but in that brief good season
under the Sign of the Sun, the distribution
is resolved with good humour and great precision;
as if, indeed, the sight of water filling the hollows
tempered their spirits to gentleness, as if the hard

core and rumble and lack of giving way, the issue
resolved only by groan and crack and fissure,
were a thing of the long dead.
Whence, in every Northern head,
a dream of the short season of impartial weights
and measures, of the time when plenty warrants
justice and generosity; their passion
for administration and their objective eye
being no more than a dream of the sun,
which they carry with them wherever they go.
As for those who stay at home, they speak hard words
the rest of the year, and reconstitute themselves
into the ancient battle lines of ice and land.
And their poetry, written under the threat
of the Glacier, is solid and hard and pitiless
as blue ice, sharp as icicles; sometimes it has
a kind of mad humour aimed at nothing,
like a man laughing to himself in his shack
in the heart of winter, under the influence
of an immature distillation of barley ...

4. News From The Capital

What kinds of feelings are left smouldering now
in the hearths of the hearts of the population
of the Capital?
The great questions have been
exhausted by thunderous answers,
and being for the thousandth time
reasserts itself as a dull pain.

There's nothing new,
no new exciting rhythm to infer
from the many scrolls or broadsheets
they're bringing out each day under the wall
where the market gathers now –
under the Wall of Scrolls
as it's come to be called,
each parchment dense in a double sense
of crammed with hieroglyphs and packed
with profundities – under the Wall
where apples from the South and all
the suspect gew-gaws of the North are sold;
from these places where a plague
is said to rage come scant
luxuries of merchants
to whom gatekeepers turn,
with connivance of the authorities,
the blindest of blind eyes.
And children play ball against the Wall
beside the Old Cathedral of Sighs,
chased by demented deacons of sorrow,
under the Wall where the Hall
of Faiths has opened a restaurant
serving a tea imported from
the dominant creed's motherland;
the sweetest tea by acclamation
of the scriveners' feet, and not a seat
for such unlikely hacks as me
who believe in telling the truth
once in a while, when the fit
is on them, knowing the city has gone
to seed from the absence of good commerce
with the country, and a few mandarins
are sustaining this predicament
for fear of surrendering their status,
which is founded on a fiction of disease :

call it the Fall, as they do in the Hall,
or the Plague, as they do in the Chambers,
or, as the scriveners do, the Nameless Affliction,
since it rhymes with their fey sense of dereliction
or their general lack of conviction.
Children play ball against the Wall
with the same indefatigability
as scriveners scrawl out their scrolls
under the Wall, as edicts to circumvent
the infiltration of the Plague
are passed in the Chambers of the embers
of good government, as tea in endless gallons drips
from the blocked spouts of teapots into the cups
of the wraiths in the Hall of Faiths,
and there's prayer for deliverance in the air
around the Old Cathedral of Sighs,
and no one really lives, though no one dies.

5. The Myth Of The North

This Northern thing goes back a long time,
necessity was the mother of our invention.
The scrawny fruit-begrudging trees, the soil
that was tundra for half the year. And so on.
(The last thing any Northerner wants to do is whine).
We had to survive or die, and as a result,
we more than survived. We became sharper than all.
And if we possess any talent that
gives people pleasure but is of no earthly use,

such as poetry or music, we don't revel in it,
as Southerners do, for its own sake, but have the sense
to surround it with an aura of mystique,
literally to *manage* it in the only way
such ephemera can usefully be handled,
by witholding it and spreading deliberate rumours
about its excellence until someone
of great consequence, who has everything else,
has got to hear of it and thinks his life
will be dull without it. In this way, our poetry
is held more in esteem than Southern singing,
which is on the lips of every Liu and Li,
though the poetry is no better than the singing.
(In fact, our best judges say privately,
and off the record, that the songs are more *inspired*.)
It is of the essence of our people
that they can convert something useless into bread;
hence the famous story of the Northerner who rented
his land for *half* the year to a Southerner.
Already, we occupy the vast majority
of positions in the administration
outside the capital. It is only a matter of time
before the scales of beleaguerment fall from the eyes
of the government and they see how much they need us.
In the end, our total control of the land
will happen by default, through our being what we are
due to our unpropitious climate, and through the fact
that fruit has always dropped into the others' mouths.

6. The Song Of The Rotten Apple.

Here let me sing among the cartwheels
on the side of the road to the ruined cities
where a plague of being forgotten lays
the land to waste, and a singer
no longer listened to
knows no difference between
the silence of his song
and the silence before and after.

Let me sing of this new word, *tension*,
a warp in people's shoulders;
neither to bloom nor fade
but be indeterminate, and wait
for something that never happens;
desire outrageously solidified,
a tower trying to penetrate
the empty air.

Here is a listless city that grew fat
in its own eyes, out of time.
Where the great songs were sung
to the creaking of cartwheels
and piled in the mind's granaries,
a plenty as endless
as water over waterfalls
on bright bodies.

This is not like an old song
going from quietness to quietness.
This is a song that has begun
out of the silence of the unheard
to end a shout in the night
from a warped face.
And between the silence and the shout,
a plague of events that happen by stealth.

And this is neither a song
of pillage nor of murder.
This is a song of cartwheels
that fall from carts and are not replaced,
and the slow rotting of grain
that has been gathered.
A song of the blight that infects the eye
of power: the Song of the Rotten Apple.

4. GETTING AWAY

A STAB OF SUNLIGHT

Not for the first time this morning's sun
has cut through clouds and struck the curtain,
but this is the first time it's struck me,
spreading its light on possibility.

And through the breach the sunlight has revealed
in the wall between me and the world,
I see a prisoner escape, and trees
that were waiting in dusty pictures
for money to grow on branches
transplant themselves into a nearby wood
and spread their winged memories far and wide.

And an old woman who nearly died
of praying over a salmon cutlet
has eaten well and thinks of going out.

In a stab of sunlight she's aware
of life and gossip in her ear.

FRIESLAND SEQUENCE

1. Heerenveen.

Everything behind it was so shaky,
so near the brink of collapse,
everyone trying so hard
in the light of whatever madness

that the train is speeding towards Heerenveen
through flat country with woodland contours,
past geese farms and canals
and sails moving through pastures.

Heerenveen, Heerenveen, say the wheels
as if they said *Nowhere, Nowhere.*
The child is sitting asleep
between his father and mother

the arrow of whose longing is a train
homing on Heerenveen
and what will prove to be
the needed kind of station –

empty and sleepy in the heat
of a mid-July afternoon
on the outskirts of a town
with hinterland of forest and silence.

2. Wadden Zee.

The word was already ringing in my ears
as we drove to the ferryport near Holwerd
to sit and look at the Wadden Zee:
moeilijk, the bespectacled proprietor
had told me in the Holwerd antique shop;
moeilijk, incomprehensible, repeated
like the striking of one of his antique clocks
through our non-conversaion; *moeilijk*,
a bespectacled man becoming a clock tower
before my eyes. And *moeilijk* again
is what I think now of what I saw then,
seated in a car, looking at the Wadden Zee.
A photograph taken on colour film
lies on my desk a monochrome,
an old-fashioned sepia print of Friesland coast
where, as Davies said, everything looks the same.
I can hardly tell the sand apart from the sky
except in the foreground by the dark lines
of breakwaters, and it's impossible
to tell if there's a sea.
Moeilijk: and inconclusive nothingscape,
a country without a language
in which, as you travel, you lose your own.
Moeilijk: a tolling bell on the wind
that is blowing here in its own quarter.

3. At Moddergat.

I'm standing on top of the dike
near a monument to drowned
fishermen, below me
on one side a row of houses
and on the other side, beyond
the dike's hemline of mussel shells,
a *moeilijk* waste of sand.

But look – the nothingscape
has blossomed over there
into a field of sheep
and cattle, where a windblown patch
of sunlight drags its anchor.

4. The Dike.

Landward, the dike is sheep's pasture;
its seaward side is hard –
a sloped cycling track,
a gull's graveyard.

Above the flap of wind
on the dike near Harlingen,
I hear a seabird piping
night-noises of my son.

5. A Memory of Harlingen.

In the oblivion of a café's
cool interior, a bewhiskered waiter
has lost his memory of two tourists
and their baby at an open-air table
and their time-worn order of French onion soup.

Chiselled from Simon Vestdijk's fiction,
a gauche schoolboy presides
over the nearby canal bridge
where old men while away the hot
humid afternoon on wooden benches,
watching a summer bohemia.

On the harbour esplanade, beside the dike,
genuflecting on a tall pedestal
and shrunken to half-size, another youngster
pushes his thumb against a concrete slab
and hollers a warning back towards the town,

over the bristling masts of schooners
and yachts, over the absentmindedly
ornate houses, the motionless water
of the peasoup-green canal where algae
are dreaming a sluggish well-fed dream
of white clouds and the tops of trees.

EPIPHANY IN BUFFALO

The skywards leap of thirty, thirty-five
buildings or so, and I'm being driven through
downtown Buffalo, massive, impressive,

but unlike downtown Chicago
in that there are some burnt-out lesser shells
amid Sullivan's teetering art decor

and Rockerfeller's ones, which go for style
less than for height and mass; then suddenly
we have rounded a corner into a stall

of traffic, and as if the scene
had been laid on by the city fathers
this spring Sunday, especially for me,

I see a gun in a holster, so near
I could touch it only for the glass
of the side-window: its owner's grip is far

from paternal on the shoulder of a black
youngster with handcuffed hands behind his back.

IN OREGON

(for Ger Killeen and Kate Saunders)

(1)

If you could speak of a town ten miles long
as being hemmed in, then Lincoln City was,
between the Pacific and the forest hills
of Oregon: "Ten miles of hotdog stalls",
as Kate, herself an Oregonian,
described the hastily-improvised look
of that long street, a wild-west city made
from the meeting up of several wild-west towns.

So now you drive, rather than walk, to showdowns.

(2)

And the Lincoln City post office assistant
was straight out of *American Gothic*
(which I saw later in Chicago):
a dour fundamentalist without her pitchfork,
but for all I knew she had hidden it
under the counter and would impale
heretics who believed in such things
as the International Express Mail;
and when the computer proved her orthodox,
I worried about unseen prongs.

(3)

The house is surrounded by hills
of Hemlock and Douglas Fir,
and on a platform outside
at night, a pair of raccoons clamber
for scattered food, wearing their burglar's masks,
their bushy tails striped like a convict's suit.
Bowing and scraping across the stage
in a fearful instinctive dance,
they gather up peanuts and lift them
to eat in cupped miniature hands
like humans drinking water from a spring,
actors acknowledging an ovation,
blowing kisses to a delirious night
of bears, coyotes, mountain lions,
and drunken redneck loggers poised to shoot
at roadsigns, guns protruding from their holsters.

(4)

And a gun protruded from the holster
of a wild-eyed logger in blue denim
I saw striding among Safeway consumers
who were meekly carrying Easter provisions
from store to car: *what is he looking for,
this tall wild-eyed cowboy in blue?*

Have I stepped into a Western?

(5)

And the radio says the Blazers have won
again, and further down the coast,
in Los Angeles, the police have been
caught red-handed on video at last
beating a black traffic offender senseless,

and I'm peering through dim binoculars
from the veranda of Kate's mother's house,
watching a darker smudge on the bottle-
green of the end-of-March Pacific
that might turn out to be a killer whale.

(6)

And finally, those land-cousins
of yellow waterflowers
I photographed with my cheap camera
beside Slab Creek in twilight downpours,

the spring bloom of a weed
called Skunk Cabbage, in the field
near the children's school founded
by ageing Hippies: the shot that failed.

MARGARITAS

In some arty-decor friendly-neighbourhood sidestreet
not far from the John Hancock Centre towering
over Chicago at Michigan and Chestnut,
a horse of a different colour in the uncertain sunshine
of an early April afternoon, I drank Margaritas:
tequila tang met salt tang of the glasses rim
on my lips, a silver sun at the world's end.
Salt tang and tequila, bite of lime and cold of ice,
and the husky voice of a plump but petite waitress :
"Why d'ya wanna *buy* food, when it's *complimmenary?*"
Hot chilli sauce on Buffalo chicken wings, in Chicago,
the friendly-neighbourhood voices of people who greet
one another every day, young white women bantering
with black men, and the occasional cadaverous
eyes of a down-and-out watching across the way
and waiting for eye-contact to encourage him
to come and introduce his needs at the railing
that separates the sidewalk from the tables
of Margarita-drinkers outside a Mexican café
on a street that runs parallel with Lake Shore Drive,
where I among them, conscious of the towering height
of the John Hancock Centre, Chestnut St, a horse
of a different colour, am sinking into silver light,
tequila and salt meeting at the world's rim.

THE DOVES OF PEACE

In Greenwich Village on this Saturday
morning, it seems something has gone astray
that people are in no hurry to find,
pensively ambling through a spring weekend.
Apple and cherry blossom in Washington Square:
A World Free of War and the Threat of War
is what the thin bespectacled woman seeks,
but she'll be wearing her placard for weeks,
months, years, under the reproof of the stone
stare of the gentleman in period gown
on the pillar of the arch she's standing near
in my photograph, before the doves of peace are more
than emblematic, peace real as the city breed
hopping about her feet – the ones the tourists feed.

AMERICA

America swallowed me like a fly alighting
at just the right moment on a dinner sandwich
in *The Daily Planet*, Burlington, Vermont,
and processed me through the tract of its travelways.
I remember the thisness and thatness of conversations,
my own voice breaking out of my soundproofed head
whenever the door was opened, and how it spun
most lucratively, on certain special occasions,
more fares and pocket money to be swallowed up
in their turn by distances and beer and bourbon.
Racing my last dollar to my next destination,
the over-indulgence of the night before
never quite finding me pipped at the post,
though sometimes it was that kind of photo-finish
which is the bane of cab-drivers and waitresses.
And here must be inserted a word of thanks
to those remote-sounding professors, my mentors,
who, despite sounding remoter with each new day
of my often overstayed welcome, managed
to know of a travel bureau on the other side of town
where a vociferous patriot wearing a yellow ribbon
on her breast could fix you up with a bargain flight
from the East Coast to the West or the other way
(and the sooner the better by silent agreement).
I remember breaking through to the Pacific
at Neskowin, Oregon, getting sunburnt there;
the elk stew and cheap brandy of the following
four days of rain in a friend's house among the firs.
And looking up at some worker
on the top of a building in Chicago,
thinking he's going to fall and drinking more
as an antidote to inverted vertigo.
Mostly I remember a round table discussion
of the excellent quality of my Irish shoes
with American poets in *The Ice Palace*
on the shores of Lake Champlain as I scrutinized
the curious tailpiece of a New England clam
and painstakingly peeled off its black condom.

GETTING AWAY

As it was in the beginning,
is now, and ever shall be:
the first sight of the sea,
that primitive horizon of events,
the *I remember* preceding memory.
Standing stones and falling rocks,
landmarks surviving the flux
of ancient expenditure and creed.

Windblown flowers bordering a holiday
home with a glimpse of ocean
from a breakfast window: getting away
from contemporary immolation
to a stillness of two weeks
by standing stones and falling rocks.

SETTING OUT FOR LA ROCHELLE

Everything as it should be:
a day beginning in sun
and French countryside, the green
shoots of corn, the vines, the clock-wise
heads of sunflowers in fieldfuls
turned towards us or away,
markets full swing in villages:
Hinyin lap-a-lap La Rochelle!

Morning, beginning, driving
to an elsewhere place with a new
passenger whose morning you
have entered into and share;
each morning new when the sun
shines on the unfamiliar,
which is often the long-forgotten:
Ganyan goan the Fench Car!

Mid-morning stop in a narrow street
among the shutters' open leaves
and openwork of window-rails;
a table in a small hotel's
courtyard, with café au lait
in bowl-sized cups reminding me
what was is elsewhere still:
Hinyin lap-a-lap La Rochelle!

9th July 1992

SKETCHES OF A FRUIT-SELLER

(1)

Stooped with the weight of two full bags,
a tall gaunt figure drags
himself past sunbeds, as the rented sun
dips into another afternoon
of weekly and fortnightly leases.
Among the rows of gleaming bodies
stretched here motionless, face up or down,
in varying degrees of tan and burn,
naked except for thongs
disappearing between buttocks, covering
crotches, the figure chants, *Banana,*
naranja, melón, coco, papaya:
a hungry seller bringing fruit
to an oversupplied market.

(2)

Banana, naranja, coco, papaya, melón,
chants the dark figure moving among
the bright bodies: *papaya, coco,*
naranja, melón, banana – an echo
from a distant time or world, a coldness
in the lost quality of the voice
causing a moment's dislocation
as if a mental shadow crossed the sun.

5. TOWARDS THE END AND THE BEGINNING

VOICES OF SOUTH AFRICA

1.

The day I was married to the Veldt,
the preacher in the pulpit
wielded the Black Book,
and told me in so many words
that if I ever proved
unfaithful, I should break my neck.

No sin of wife-buying stains
my Christian conscience:
I paid no bride-price for my bride
who was created from my side
and playfully rolled away
as far as the eye could see
no smoke from another man's chimney.

And she was the High Veldt, free
of mosquito and tse-tse fly.

*

The day I was married to the Veldt,
I swore with a bible in one
hand, and in the other a gun,
to protect her with my life
against all enemies
and British euphemisms:

"restless natives" indeed!
To think God's very seed
could be put on a par
with hottentot and kaffir!

I am the Boer,
farmer and marksman,
the Voortrekker in his laager,
murderous in all sincerity.

2.

... Meanwhile we British continued to exercise our native intel-
ligence by playing one side off against the other, dealing in promises
of convenience and guarantees like colanders.

We have been called a nation of shopkeepers, and are certainly
adept at window-dressing.

Like our flag, we waved this way and that: convinced of the
essential benevolence of our shifting policies, but reluctant to trouble
the Exchequer with the cost of any extravagant goodness, we re-
mained bricoleurs with a flair for the makeshift combination of un-
stable elements.

We have gone down in history (which was largely written by
ourselves) as those who tried to restrain the crushing hand of the Boer
in favour of gentler, piecemeal methods of pulverisation.

3.

When you have lived in this country as long
as I have, history is a short space
that requires some adjustment of thinking,

and perhaps we were too slow to adjust
to the crowded timetable of progress
from the arrogance of the eternal land
that shaped our customs and our jealousies.

Progress! the cunning shadow that gained substance
by fattening like a tapeworm in our bellies,
the fluke that lay in wait on the kiss
of equivocal treaties and promises,

progress that gave us a Book of Patience
in return for our living and our lands.

Now nothing is eternal any more
except hunger; even a dog
hungers to be a Child of the Stars.

Listen to what I have to say:
I have a rifle in my hands.

A MOMENT UNDER SIEGE

(written on the occasion of Limerick's Treaty 300 Celebrations, 1991)

1. The Siege Mentality.

The sun has risen and revealed a breach
in the wall of your life: the new
besiegers breaking through,
and nothing for it but to fight –
hand to hand combat
in a dawn of realization.

And through such competition you progress,
everyone against his neighbour's fortress;
so many powder wagons to be blown
sky-high, so many breaches
to fill before you prematurely meet
the dole queue or your Maker;
and after one siege train, another,
and then one more, *ad infinitum:*

wondering where you'll find the time,
despite it all, to celebrate
the present moment and the leaping salmon
seen through an eye of stone

before that other moment of pontoons
and treachery encroaches;
one of the kind
that ferried Ginkel's army to our side
three centuries ago, and caught us standing round
as you do now by Sunday chapel gates,
talking about a football game;

a moment that made null and void
the women's courage on the counterscarp,
when they fought with broken bottles against progress.

Always so many breaches to be filled,
so many siege trains to be blown away,

wondering where you'll ever find
the time to rest your eye
on the magic moment of the waterhen,

her deft movement over a pool of twilight.

2. The Status Quo

Now everywhere shrewd people map
their lives out with precision:
self-interest separating grain
from chaff, a realizable hope

from an utopian dream.
Everywhere now there's definition
of what can and can't be done –
a new division of the kingdom

its line of demarcation clear
between the habitat of those
with future possibilities,
and the country of Despair

whose natives, in their continuous present,
are pacified by videos.
The good news leers from the front
pages of all the papers

as it grinned in 1691
out of the *London Gazette* :
the underdog is down
again, and committees prevaricate.

3. An Utopian Dream.

At last, to all inheritors of our wars,
to the forward-lookers and the here-and-now,
I say, who am three centuries dead,
find time to celebrate the present,
but not the present dispensation
where emigrants make room
for buildings, and a river that fed
so many is a trickle to the sea.
Build something bigger than divisions,
to keep wild geese at home
with waterhens, salmon in every fridge!
And let it be a solid bridge
of stone, that through the present's eye
you may look on the future
secure in your identity, like water
that moves but holds a still reflection.

ASTRONOMY LESSONS

1. The District Nurse

Nodding in his chair in the early afternoon,
the district nurse is trying to stay awake
as the old woman makes her way
up the path to his collection of shacks.
In the blinding heat, she plays tricks on his eyes –
a shape-changer dwindling to a black ribbon
that flutters in a non-existent wind.
But she could become a small tornado
or the living model of a spiral nebula
for all he cares: he knows in a few seconds
she'll re-materialize as a patient
with some complaint for which he has no remedy –
call it war or sickness or old age
or the grinding down of the universe,
it doesn't matter. It transpires
she's looking for advice about three tablets
clutched in her fist. He observes that the back
of her hand is densely, minutely webbed
like a satellite photograph of the Great Plains
crossed by the rivers of her veins.
The three tablets, which she bought that morning
in the market, are of three different sizes.
The district nurse uncradles
his rifle and leans it against the wall
(you can never be sure with apparitions,
no matter how long they take to get
from the burnt-out stables that mark the middle distance
to the shade of his ramshackle porch).
Adjusting his hat, he looks the old woman
in the eyes. Not without sympathy, he looks
at the old woman suffering from the shock
of war and the grinding down of her universe,
and cups the hand holding the three unequal tablets

in his own. Slowly, he explains to her
that everything, of course, is relative,
even the speed of retreating galaxies,
but if she takes the small tablet to be the moon,
the big one is the sun, and the middle one
the earth: the earth goes round the sun, like this,
and the moon goes round the earth, like this; and for all
the good these tablets will do her, she might as well
learn a few true facts of astronomy.
She has walked ten miles for these tablets and this
advice. She will return this evening
through bandit country, and the district nurse,
having polished his rifle, will retire
to the living quarters behind
his dispensary with its out-of-date
medicine in cobweb-covered cabinets
and its needles lying in dust-filled sinks.
There he will wash and eat, and then
he will read deep into the night, jerking alert
out of force of habit at the smallest sounds,
but omnivorous for all that: he wants to know
what's happening at the other end
of the universe, at the beginning of time.

2. How to Convert Light into Dark Matter

Take the food from the body,
take the flesh from the ribs,
take the hope from the child,
take the pride from the man,
take the child from the mother,
take the love from the heart,
take the truth from the explanation,
take the speed from the remedy:

sit back, and watch the stars.

THE MUSSEL-EATERS OF ANTWERP

Crouched under tiers of architecture,
they're about their business by six o'clock,
these mussel-eaters of Antwerp
oblivious in street-level restaurants
of the weight of elegance above them –
turrets, cupolas, wedding-cake gables,
bare-bottomed goddesses and heroes
held in suspension on ornate facades.

And in a café near the cathedral,
amid the mock-devout decor's
garish litany of saints in plaster,
a skinny waitress serves a fat high priest
of mussel-cult apostacy
who sits among the Sacred Hearts and Martyrs
using a mussel shell to spoon
his way through a small black cauldron.

If it sounds in season, and at six o'clock,
the last trumpet will not distract
the mussel-eaters of Antwerp crouched
under the architecture as it falls:
smitten by bare-bottomed goddesses
crashing through ceilings, or Virgins
toppling from pedestals, they'll die
in a bliss of mussel-concentration.

CLEARINGS

After the clearing of wild gardens
or the shelling of besieged cities,
as swathes of light and shadow bathe
the heaps of fallen things
with timelessness and truth,
only the few remain upright:
rose bushes, buildings in the sun's last rays.

Later they too will be drawn
into the general condition,
and that by which they stand out now
be seen as a deceit
of self-containment in the aftermath.
Already no longer shrubs or streets
stunned motionless as in a photograph,

they show their aptitude for falling in
with the fallen majority;
and this is no longer a pause
in the clearing of a garden or a city
but something returning to the inert
undifferentiated heart
of darkness and beginning.

A RUMOUR OF SPIRIT

I'm researching a rumour of spirit
in a library of metal-plated shelves.
Fluorescent tubes of light are set to cool
in metal grids that cling to a blue ceiling.
The wall beside me is half-stripped of plaster,
an authentic work-in-progress whose essence
is to reveal and yet conceal the neat
fastidious handicraft of red brick.
Under its chalky surface what protects us
from the spirit's enemy, the summer day's
persistent heaviness arousing flesh
to seek a key, an entry point into
its old density and concentration
among disjunctive individuals
that to and fro in torrid heat outside,
a happy, brief togetherness of atoms,
is brick upon mortared building brick.
We live in the age of repetition,
as Warhol's reproducible Marilyn
has proved, while the unique original
overdoses on the absence from itself.
In every library in the universe,
a calendar open at May and June
has a picture of ringed plovers on a beach,
the female sitting over speckled eggs.
There's a thistle in the foreground and the shingle
is littered with scallop and mussel shells.

EARTHLINGS

Having beamed myself back up to where I am
from where they flounder, all I can report
about earthlings to my superiors
is that they are a sorry lot.
I am bound to say that their method
of measuring time (the product
of inadequate brain-power) is so crude
as almost to defy explanation.
They have this notion of succession
of events, which they abstract
as a series of finite points
or numbers, whose centre is called *now*.
Measuring proceeds backwards or forwards
from this centre; the forward direction
is called *future*, the backward *past*.
Thus *five years past* is measured
towards some putative Beginning
according to the revolution
of their planet round their sun,
and this is a *point in time* which they regard
in some way as extinguished, while
five years from now, projected
towards some imagined Ending, is considered
(incomprehensibly) not to exist *as yet*,
to be in some sense out of reach, but not
quite as extinguished, *for present purposes*,
as five years past. From the imagined point
where they now think they are,
they experience perturbations when
they look backwards or forwards,
and these perturbations differ
qualitatively according to direction:
the past is often viewed as a condition
that obtained before the occurrence
of certain undesirable events;

and they distress themselves with the absurdity
of wishing to be back at a point
they believe has been irrevocably extinguished.
And while we know that this arises from
the initial misconception, namely
their notion of linear progression,
just try expressing that to them
in their kind of elementary language!
The perturbation concerning the future
is called *to forbode*, or *to make plans*;
sometimes it is called *looking forward*;
or *dreading*; or *hoping*; in many ways
this notion of the future is related
to the notions of *improvement*
and *disimprovement*, while the notion
of the past is related to the notions
of *perfection* and *innocence*. And both
are sometimes related to the idea
of *nothing – non-existence*. None of these
notions would have the power they do
over humans were it not that they are tied
up with another cardinal idea:
that of *having* or *possessing*, and with
its opposite, that of *not having* or *losing*.
They look backwards, for example, to what
they've lost or think they've lost, especially
innocence, *promise, opportunity*.
They look forward with forboding to the loss
of what they think they now have, or with hope
towards some imagined gain. The only ones
who are moving in a manner which suggests,
even remotely, some semblance of knowledge
of the true relations of the cosmic flux,
make, as they go, a curious eruptive noise
which shakes them from within and causes
contortions of the face and posture,
shortness of breath and water from the eyes.

RECOURSE, RESOURCE

Along a dusty road through a green desert
where nothing's happened for half a century,
I'm driving my brindled bardic cow
back to the birthplace of its divinity.

A bloom of sloes, a stain of blackberries,
a weary statement of the lie of fields
viewed from a rusted gate,
trees printed cloudily on late summer heat,

my dry-milked cow of inspiration
ambling distracted by grassy margins,
and the road leading to a hump-backed bridge
with the waters of nothingness flowing beneath.

And then the pain of cold around my ankles,
and suddenly, in the shadow under the bridge,
my brain invaded by the force of water
in a gibberish of dissolution

passing into shadows and brightnesses
with the brindled molecules of the cow
and through the water into layers of darkness
and the black holes of foundering galaxies.

To rise again and see for the first time
nothingness singing the shape of water;
and driving a full-uddered cow before me,
I step once more from the stream of origin.

6. Back Home

PETALS

On the mantlepiece of the marble fireplace
in our new house, an end-of-summer rose,
white on a thin green stem, sticks out
of a pale green miniature jar
with a few decorative brush strokes
on its squat belly. A few sprigs of leaves,
speckled with rust, are lower branches
beneath the head of this innocent triffid
inclined with a clumsy weight of petals
ready to fall from grace, to fall from the weight
of having no other place to go;
and a million blocked lives, and a million more,
are petals on waters going nowhere,
like the ones that have fallen into the bowl
I put beside the gas heater to keep
the air moist and the skin of my hands and face
from flaking. The petals of the white rose flake
away at the touch and plummet – yes, at least
in comparison with other ways I've seen
the petals of roses falling, they plummet –
past the curious *art nouveau* designs
painted in green and gold on the dark marble,
into the bowl of waters going nowhere.
Somewhere there's a word for you, even
a world for you, innocent griffins
who spring at me out of the redbrick sunsets
at the back of the house, laying me flat
as the flattest rose out of the autumn
wilderness of our new garden, the city
in heaps of loosening bricks around me.

HELPING IN THE GARDEN

I'm lopping the withered stalks of tall
unidentified flowers with a clippers
and making a heap of them on the grass
beside the flowerbed. My bent back
hurts from this unaccustomed exercise
and the fresh wind sends shivers down my spine.
Raw weather and raw humour on this late
Sunday in February – big dull clouds,
at odds with promise, moving overhead,
and my eyes creaking reluctantly open
to happenings at my feet: moist folded buds
pushing for life out of the same roots
as last year's rotten but tenacious stalks.
Peevish and in no mood for drawing morals
from such epiphanies, I'm moving
purposefully towards a cigarette
and a cup of coffee: it's all very well,
this obligatory hour of gardening,
sinking your tenuous roots back in the earth,
but the thing is to get it over with
and return to the beckoning inertia
of the fire warming up the living room.
Conor is "helping" me in the garden,
listening to a different drummer, the one
that plays sudden tattoos of inspiration
in the minds of two and a half year olds.
Daddy, I haff ta beed dem in de bin.
By the time I look up he has gathered
an ungainly bundle of stalks in his arms,
and now he's shedding them along the path
as he walks away, head down, heedless
of the paternal static increasing
in volume on his brainwave-receiver.

LINE'S ODYSSEY

(for David Lilburn)

These are outhouses poised for flight,
or tense with a force about
to spring. The country
bustles like the city,
and everything shouts its origins
in lines that will not rest
until the thrumming energy
of stillness is manifest.

This is line's odyssey
through colour's archipelago,
marks on paper that condescend
to wear the temporary mantle
of what's at hand,
shape-shifting in their elemental
permanence to become
a swollen stream, trees in a circle
of seasons, dockland;
to feed the wiry strength of marshgrass
or cut cranes down to size,
fatten to pregnancy, midwife birth.

Equal to everything on earth,
marks that remain themselves in all.

TOWARDS NIGHT AND WINTER

(after the painting by Frank O'Meara)

Carrying a bundle of autumn leaves
in the apron-fold of a blue-grey dress
down to her burning place,
she is surprised by failing light.

It's still too early for the fire to glow:
there's no more than a tongue
of autumn burnish in an altered state,
and blue-grey smoke, one chore among

many of that quotidian
and seasonal pentecost
spreading its gospel of ghost,
the ghosts of colours and differences,

and she has been caught there
between the wicket and the pool
against a background light of gables,
in the act of fading.

FOR CONOR ON THE APPROACH
OF HIS THIRD BIRTHDAY

Today, it looks like you'll have recovered
from three weeks of being out of sorts,
enough to be able to celebrate
your birthday in the company of your peers.
We've been too trusting of inoculations:
by the time we brought you to the doctor
his diagnosis was facile and almost
superfluous, lifting your vest aside
to reveal that final stage of Rubella,
the blotchy archipelago. That was last night;
this morning your skin was clear and your eyes
were brighter, you were more cheerful and giddy
as I dressed you, and you finished your bowl
of *beckett* to the last residual
spoonful of milk. You didn't understand
why we were full of praise for you, and more
tolerant than usual: we knew
that for the past three weeks you had been less
not yourself than might have been expected
for a child going through a grey tunnell
of unstable temperatures, swollen glands,
various infections, a leaking nose,
and such other discomforts as would bring
the whinge-factor into play with a vengeance
in lesser mortals. Congratulations, son;
you have come out of one of nature's mindless
initiation rites with flying colours,
with something approaching grace, into a bright
mid-April morning: let us stand together
here on the pavement in front of your creche
for a few minutes, while the cherry trees
laden with blossom take my breath away,
and a goods train rumbling towards the cement factory
takes yours, crossing the space between
the houses up at the end of the street.

EPILOGUE

How do you find your true voice,
the one they'll call *the real you*?
The way light comes to rest on roofs of slate
and is at rest there, having found
its proper place at last,
and the slates no longer cold,
bathed in gentle light, their only one,
never better nor more true
to themselves than showing how light can rest.

How do you find your true voice
without the other who is also you?
A car moves tranquilly along
the road down by the sea,
and only reflection tells you that inside
is likely to be much hot air
of purpose, business. And somehow
the Tao is always a mile down the road,
across the next bridge, like a rainbow.

Here at this window I can understand
how the elements purify, and why
they are the greatest story-tellers.
Look for a miracle and you'll find
a brightening prismatic haze
in the centre background of your picture
across the water, reaching towards the sky.
How can I find my true voice
without my other, you, my miracle?

Heinrich Böll House, Achill Island, 28 February 1993